WORLD MUSIC .

PATRICK MORRISSEY

WORLD
MUSIC

VERGE BOOKS

CHICAGO

Published by Verge Books

www.vergebooks.com

ISBN 978-0-9889885-5-2

Design and composition by Quemadura

Printed on acid-free, recycled paper

in the United States of America

Thanks to the editors of *Lute & Drum*, *The Nation*,
and *VOLT*, where some of these poems first appeared;
thanks also to the Woodland Pattern Book Center, and
especially to Jordan Dunn, for printing a letterpress
broadside edition of "Squall." Finally, thanks to
Joel Calahan for his careful help in preparing this book.

in memory of Michael O'Brien

SECOND SLEEP

SECOND
SLEEP

SECOND SLEEP

Day breaks
with the garbage

truck's beep
then dissolves

into fog, a
second sleep

cradled in diesel,
the hydraulics

churning at
some distance,

a vague dream
turning over again.

LAKE SHORE

basso
      continuo

the lake rolls
      against boulders,

slabs, glass and
      stone, glinting

shards of the
      grid sifted

smooth and
      collectible

among girders
      a merganser

4

tilts its head
    and decamps

northeastward

WELTER

Sun slants
on milky

swells, ducks
calm atop

a welter
of shadows.

Water
knuckles

across
the rocks, a

barrelhouse
combo

falling apart.

ARTICULATE

a fluent en-
closure, the

wrist swivels
and nods,

silent on its
stem of bones

GRAFFITO

always hungry,
    never guilty

neon scrawls
    along concrete

the all-night
    tremble and hum

of halogen, some-
    body's ghost

echoes down
    the viaduct

a craving traced
    by a hand cast out

FOR ED ROBERSON

BICYCLIST

He wobbles on
his bicycle,

steadies, threads
an *s* through

traffic, clank
of gears, a chain

around his
person, a

person around
its breath.

FIGURES

Bundles, piss
bottles, bags
of bread, a nest
inarguably composed.
He writes down
what he hears,
guarding his stash
of pages, face
a rictus one
minute, rolling
vacant the next.
He would seem
beyond us,
but he is
always here.

She draws
herself up
into light
she lets fall

across cheek-
bones, chin,
chest, palms
opening out

a shadow
drops from
feet to head,
sun, cloud

then sun
again, her
eyes held still
behind lids.

Agitated
then matter
of fact, he has
a story to tell,
something that
happened a long
time ago. His
hands curl and
leap, crackling
syllables, maybe
a sentence,
then just a string
of strangled
names, that thing
burrowed down
in the dark
pushing itself
up, gasping
for air.

At my desk
again, watching
a shadow
sweep the page

I mouth the
words, turning
them over by
hand and tongue

noiselessly
I think until
your voice
carries in

from another
room, *Hey,*
were you saying
something?

SURFACES

A contrail
dissipates

to white
cursive

loops, then
nothing—

flat, noise-
less, no

telling how
far off—

out past
the breakers

gravity
looms up

and washes
under.

AFTER THE STORM

Pocked limestone
corners, flecks,
detonated lake-
bed flung afield
and terrace swept
clean of brush by
the horizon whipped
into angled fits.

A little wren
steals among

odd synthetic
neon bits, a

rusted flange
and someone's

sandal plowed
ashore, relict

wares seeding
sudden furrows.

Maple sapling
snapped,
       run
with ribbon, as if
a cassette had un-
strung all its songs.

FOR PETER O'LEARY, 11.1.14

TRANSIT

Winter, the bus
crowded, hushed

charge rippling
along the velour

and plastic interior,
a warm murmur

out of which
a voice detaches

itself and rises,
as if to disembark—

*I just don't know
what to do with myself*

SQUALL

sky like television
static, familiar

bricks, windows
snowed out

a row of trees
dissolves in the glow

bits of signal
ticking at the sill

GUIDO'S VIRTU

a scalpel-
    song, love's cut

forms in light
    forms of light

edge slices
    through edge, glass

slightly cracked
    that makes the

light strike just
    visible

SOURCES

Blackbirds drop
in threes from
a cornice
perch, shadows
following
sources down
washed sunlit
bricks. It's late
afternoon,
lengthening
angles, some
old pages
torn loose, held
together
a moment
midair, then
drafted a-
way, turning
noiselessly
to catch in
trees and wires.

HEAT WAVE

offshore haze
a membrane

settled where
atmosphere

swaps with
surface, cirrus

thinning
to blue, all

edges feathering
the depths

windless, a
list of things

continuously
not getting

done, janitors
hosing down

the sidewalks,
a spider

high on the wall
in early light

felt in
the room,

a tape hiss,
minimum

ambient
charge, its

medium
thickening

with tiny
shifts, a

tremble
in the array

sweating all
night, fan's

whirr
circulating

solid air,
our dreams

turning
fitfully

through
each other

SWIMMING

some voices, a
   laugh, traffic
      murmur drifting

over, water's
   rim broken
      by a buoy

aloft, a lake
   bird oars
      itself forward,

tumbledown
   rocks and pilings,
      breadth shifting

even light,
   an edge to
      push off from

FOR MARIA FAHEY

EVENING NEWS

Silhouettes
    flicker blue

in tiny
    rooms, evening

news, voices
    piped in from

elsewhere to
    witness, as

I do, at
    a window,

saying, *Now*
    back to you.

LEFT OPEN

A window
left open

to move the air,
I wake into

a gamut, jack-
hammer, siren,

gray sigh
of transit.

The blind
man adheres
to concrete,
propped un-
evenly on one
cane, sweeping
ahead with
the other, fellow
pedestrians
eddying, filling
in his wake.

Glass, asphalt,
October's all

blocked out,
blue lifting

almost free
of the grid,

a curl of
laminate

caught
at the edge.

A band of clouds
lit pink, long over
the river's brackish
lower expanses

concentration gradient
constant, changing

choppers and ferries
to Jersey and back.

Elderly friends
exchange a chuckle,
testing their lines.

A panicked crab
clatters across
the concrete pier.

Reporters, vans
and their antennae

tuned to the
network, dead

air waiting
for word,

the microphone's
foamy hush.

"very concerned" about
the virus, carefully following
protocols, modifiers
deployed for protective
emphasis

scaffold of
pipes, scaffold
of bones, jointed
lines the solid
air hangs upon

every angle
an opportunity
to sound out

In the gallery
we gather around,

fascinated
by the depth

in a rectangle.
We shift aspects,

we ask each other
how it works.

Something between
a figure and a form
held almost moving

along a vague
horizon, no, a
gradient of blues

and browns, thin
wash of green out
to corner and edge.

Droll, silver-
haired, he

claps and turns
a two-step, a

laugh for his
somber son,

no, it's his
boyfriend.

Today the river
seems a steadiness
of little winks

until at odd
intervals a sudden
trough slaps up

against the wall,
vague agency,
sustained delay.

corner of gray
sky through
the window
and rows
of windows

afternoon
inching across
the avenue

As if from
rotating speakers

atop a moving
vehicle, a sound

like world music
rises, curling

into abstraction.

Lit colors stream
the avenues, around
corners, a net of
itineraries spreading
hushed behind
night glass, a fluency
of right angles.

Abstracted voice
keeps coming

back without
a body yet

still crackling
across the train's

faint speaker,
familiar tones.

Ducks, vagrants,
crumbling docks,

a flock of creative
professionals

lofted above
countertops

all along
the Hudson.

Invisible, living
threat, tiny insistent
monster come in
through cracks and
errors just to tell us
how present else-
where always is.

a sink or
window almost

alive, ghosted
with light,

slight intention

One slide for
another, a book

becomes a
window, a shell

an ear, a room
becomes a plane

of slight shifts,
leaves, the frame

constant, holding
all its ghosts.

Somehow some
hydrangeas are
holding on, last
leaves turned out
toward what light
slips around the
building's corner.

The train scans
half-collapsed brick

mills and projects,
windows splintered

and staved, crows
trading inside for out.

calendar, patched
together, the days

fluttering
in excess of
any schedule

Riding out, I look
through my own face.

The city gives way
to a broader complex:

power lines, meridians
the clouds shift across.

HELD
CONSTANT

Radio voices, a truck heaves, the grid of roofs and bricks,
 each morning

The dream splits into specifics, a labyrinth's every edge
 glimpsed in light

Birds the size of fists perched above the doorframe startle
 as I step out

Waiting at the curb, horizon swept clean, gray either side
of the crease

Schools shuttered, "at risk" kids shifted into transit,
ways marked "safe passage"

Try to see the next thing while all the rest tumble in at
odd angles

Port of Chicago pouring steam, water's tonnage turning
in its bed

Please no eating, smoking, littering, gambling, or radio
playing

As if enameled, as if the rule, horizon's water held
constant

Through walls my neighbor stomps and screams, *You have to treat me better, asshole*

Inexorable bass below traffic's drone, snatch of scratchy treble

Mute clouds, their blunt margins, waiting for someone to acknowledge a grudge

Dreaming the sound of bulldozers, waking up in a
  construction site

I think out loud, *I need to get back inside my body,* try counting

The computer hums along, vague, the room holding
  itself together

Refrigerator, a man in the corner, the door on its hinges

A white sail's slow progress, unflappable, the horizon
   makes no sound

As abstract as a clock, as accurate as a radio dial

Realism's watchdog prowls the neighborhood, insisting
   again, *That's that*

This technology, heat's buzz, a thousand eyes, dreamt
   of something to touch

I hear my body humming, constant in error's every
   register

Commotion, a momentary surge, water throws a form
dissolving

Loudspeaker voices, rhapsodic, an echo overlapping its
source

If I have lapsed, if I have been inconstant, allow me to
repeat

Lake water clad in shadows rolling eastward, the brim
   of light's last laugh

She lets out his leash, jerks back at the car sound,
   attachment's rhythmic now

Asphalt darkens with rain, city bus heaving itself into
   traffic

Finance towers in fog, low overhead, now a small plane
drops below

My face in the glass gives out as light passes, breath
blurring the contours

Familiar chords heard through the floor, a song before
the words come out

Unrented rooms, windows, shadows passing time, the
    floorboards' tongue and groove

To make it all equally visible but not all at the same time

Riding the bus across neighborhoods, places felt as
    surface friction

Gulls lift, draft-drawn, slightly rigid, cries resounding off
the barriers

Scatter of light, all angles simultaneous, tiny displacements

Limestone cuts the rush, slaked gray sun glints, a tattoo in
the ear's eddy

Smokestacks black against purple clouds, the lights of
  Gary, Indiana

The news crackles and splits across bandwidths, Orpheus
  lost in a crowd

Driving across the grid, those radio towers' intermittent
  reds

Irregular, bobbing gulls or recurrent whitecaps at this
   distance

The passenger jet's slow, noiseless ascent, clouds plowing
   the horizon

Accident assumes a form and repeats in what we say
   about it

She strolls the neighborhood, proud of the voices that
   accompany her

Rows of vacants, loose teeth, crows and squirrels, economy
   off the grid

A cloud of tiny bugs, quick as pixels, catches sun then
   disappears

City geometry crumbling slowly, the lake mute,
  unpersuaded

I give him fifty cents, he gives me back a fist bump, it's
  our routine

Not "happenings" but what happens, exactly, that you
  would notice it

Born in 1982, Patrick Morrissey grew up in Andover, Massachusetts, and studied literature at Harvard and the University of Chicago. His first book of poems, *The Differences*, was published by Pressed Wafer in 2014. From 2014 to 2016, he served as poetry editor of *Chicago Review*. He lives with his wife and son in Chicago, Illinois.